Widen

A COLLECTION OF POEMS

Chris Rice

Chris Rice Books / chrisrice.com

ISBN 978-0-9973231-0-8

First Edition

Printed in the United State of America

Chris Rice Books

More information about the author is available at www.chrisrice.com

INTRODUCTION by the Author

My years as a songwriter have taught me that words are like tiny Trojan horses which, once welcomed in, can make a mighty mess of things. Sometimes they are weapons for harm, but in kinder hands with good intentions words can be life-giving. I have often been instantly undone by a song's lyrics. And how many laughs have suddenly erupted when an old poet blindsided me with a new thought!

An inner drive to communicate compelled me to my songwriting career—compressing lyrics into a melody, framing them in clumsy guitar chords or handfuls of piano keys, straining the lines through tight vocal chords, circled by a band of players, squinting at spotlights, trying to move roomfuls of friends and strangers to consider life, faith, and love, in hopefully interesting ways.

It is always about words for me. My mind won't stop playing with words. But as an introvert, face-to-face verbal exchange is not my strong suit. I find expression much more manageable from the comfortable distance of a stage or a recording studio, or from behind a computer keyboard, or by means of pen and paper.

The lure of words has drawn me to more than songwriting over the years. I have also written essays, articles, poems, and even a few short stories and longer fiction. I have been reluctant to share these beyond my family and closest friends, but now I am eager to embark on a new artistic adventure. The result is this book, a collection of ninety poems I have written over the past several years.

I grew up with the notion that 'poetry' only applied to a sentimental, mushy, flowery, cliché-filled, greeting-card manner of writing. Of course some poetry is just that, and a lot of people appreciate it. But I want to aim my writing toward more solid, charged, muscular words. Words with a chew to them. Words with depth built into them, especially in the ways they are combined (not that I achieve that goal in every poem, but I do try). A poet does far more than rhyme nice words. He tackles thoughts and viewpoints. Poetry is a vigorous game of language played between poet and reader.

The poet Samuel Taylor Coleridge defined poetry as "the best words in their best order." I like his off-the-cuff definition because it spells out freedom as well as an outright challenge to experiment with language. To combine and recombine words and thoughts until one is satisfied, even thrilled, with how they speak and sing. And with Coleridge's definition, every poet and every reader is enlisted to dive in headlong and define what 'best' means for his own soul, in his own times. I have sifted through my pile of scribblings from the past handful of years to offer you the ones I consider my best so far.

Whether you study other poets or merely dabble as I do, I hope you find in my poems the influence of some of my old-school favorites—William Shakespeare, Elizabeth Barrett Browning, Rainer Maria Rilke, William Wordsworth, Walt Whitman, and Emily Dickinson, to name just a few. Some of my poems dare to engage in time-travel conversations with these heroes. And admittedly, some of my writing borrows their archaic styles.

Shakespeare tinkered with verb tense and parts of speech to push the limits of our language and create new meanings. Browning gushed with romantic pain and hope. Rilke screamed torment and beauty into his oddly-Godded universe. Wordsworth warmly drew readers into the mystery of nature, memory, and childhood. Whitman simply turned everyone and everything into poet food. Dickinson hid and discovered gutsy meaning in simple, often quirky, language and punctuation.

What most attracts me to these poets is their ability to make me think new thoughts and see connections I never would have considered without them. Hopefully my writing will do a bit of the same for you, or lead you back to these poets or others, or compel you forward to join the conversation and write some of your own.

Upon reading and rereading (the best path into poems) you will notice some recurring themes in my writing: the natural universe, color, childhood, aging, faith, doubt, fame, time, agency, awe, and some meta, self-referential looks at the very process of writing.

I offer this poetry collection loosely. I'm not an expert poet nor an expert on any subject that I approach in these poems. I do this only for the love of words . . . as an amateur. I find comfort in some of these lines. I squirm at others. I often exaggerate. I sometimes write as other characters, expressing their feelings and not my own. I often write in outdated, long-abandoned styles, just to have fun pressuring language into the meter of bygone periods. Some poems I write in a more modern, commonplace, conversational style. I play with irony and humor. Even serious subjects are not exempt from an amusing encounter.

No reader will appreciate or agree with all of my viewpoints or methods. Each of you will have favorites and least-favorites. This is why I offer these poems loosely, as friendly gifts, with no need or expectation for you to cherish them, just to engage and enjoy the variety.

Part of the challenge and glory of poetry is that we don't often 'get it' on a first read. As readers it is up to us how much effort we put into finding a meaning. If you tire of trying or disagree with something you read, move on to another poem without fretting. Revisit it later. Discuss it with others for their insights. Or simply rip it out of the book so it doesn't ruin the rest of these poems for you.

Most importantly, this poet's intention is not the only or final meaning of his poems. You will discover more in these lines than I ever intended. I discovered this truth through decades of songwriting. We share the language, but each of us brings our personal history and perspective into the words. A poem or song will say different things to different people, including the writer. And your meaning is as valid and valuable as mine.

If I pictured myself in a particular poem's scene slouching on my stone patio, but you read yourself instead on a rickety creek-side dock, so much better! The poem did its double duty! If I smile at a childhood memory, but my account moves you to tears instead, the poem is both yours and mine. As poets and readers we share in the work of imagination and discovery. It would cheat the reader and diminish the poem for the poet to explain or defend it at every turn, so I will resist that urge.

I already sense the overwhelming privilege to stimulate thoughts and conversations by another form of writing. Mull these poems over. Wrestle with them. Squirm or find peace in them like I do. Agree or disagree with them. Underline, circle, and jot notes in their margins. Trek through them with friends and family. Teach them to your students. Start a discussion group or use this collection in your book club. Or simply enjoy some cozy bedtime reading.

I hope your eyes and souls will widen along with mine, time after time, with the thoughts I've labored to capture on these pages.

—Chris Rice

"...l'amor che move il sole e l'altre stelle."

—Dante Alighieri (Paradiso)

Widen

CONTENTS

River of Time 1

Widen 3

Squirrel Chase 4

I Aimed an Arrow Inward 5

First Flake 6

Bread, Wine, and Water 7

Tend 8

Crib 10

Stages 11

Dead Poets 13

Warm 15

I Wear My Favorites Out 16

Live to Be a Thousand 18

Curtains 20

Kindergarten 21

Rain 23

Who Has Summered at the Beach 24

Nostalgia 26

Life Science 27

Undertones 28

Neigh 29

Fame Is an Africanized Bee 31

Lies..32

Hangover 33

Exhausted Poet 35

On Time 36

Shy Poem...38

The Language of Crows...40

No More 43

One-Piece Puzzles 44

I Was Larger When a Child 45

Perfection...47

Rich Old Lady...48

Then Sings My Soul 51

What to Do with Guilt 54

First Memory 55

A Lost Art..56

Sky, the Word 58

Psalm Eighty-Eight-and-a-Half................................61

December 12 62

Do Not Write Me Larger Than I Am 63

Slow Explosion 65

Edges 66

Grace..69

Our Best Minds 70

Clues.. 72

Optimist... 73

Pillow Math 75

River Talk 76

Painter's Tantrum.. 78

You Cannot Prove.. 79

Unexplainable 81

Waves.. 82

The Poet Interrupts.. 85

Words.. 87

Impossibility Theory.. 88

Starlings 90

My Devils Sing.. 91

Dying Alone 92

Borrowed 94

Hoarder 95

I Was Just Thinking 96

Adorned.. 97

Oak in October... 99

Doubter's Prayer 101

Hindsight 103

Birthday 104

To Sun, Moon, and Men 106

The News 108

The Feel of Words 109

Too Much I Love 110

Soul 111

Just Kids 112

Mercy and Judgement 114

We Rarely Die..116

Upon Reading Wordsworth's Ode...........................117

Every Bed..118

Catharsis 119

Waking 121

Black Hole...122

The Importance of Maps..123

Cause 126

First Stone...127

The Innocence of Innocence 128

Flaunt 129

Sunlight...130

The Universe Is Bent 132

Bucket List 134

Spring 135

When I Survey 137

River of Time

I will build my cabin on a river
With a westward porch to wink goodnight
To the yawning sun in his purple bed clothes.

I will pass those star-clobbered evenings
Reading the river's moon-sparkle,
Hearing her sing all her gurgled secrets.

I will still be perched on my wooden chair
When the sun reawakens in golden robes
To the bright morning chatter of house wrens.

I will waste those lazy days pondering
How Time is like a river,
Or maybe it is not.

I will not be certain
If Time brings the future to us from upstream,
Or if Time carries us downstream toward it.

Are we fixed here on her banks
While she rushes over us, through us,
To siphon this moment into the past
Somewhere around the next bend?

Or are we the ones borne along on her currents
Like canoes, aimed and bobbing

Toward the impatient future?

Whether Time carries us
Or flows through us,
It doesn't matter to me.
I will build my cabin on a river.

Chris Rice

Widen

Create, create, create!
Rearrange the molecules
Of the already astounding universe.

Your notes, your lines, and your strokes
Spill out your awe of it,
And hint at beauties you can never outdo.
But try anyway!
At least mimic
As offerings of flattery.

Would Wolfgang or William
Have ever surmised
The strength of rolling time
To bear them entangled down centuries'
halls?
Atop boiling oceans onto alien shores?
Through electric skies
Into minds and ears and eyes
Of numberless other breathing masterpieces?

Create, I say!
An eye will widen
Because of it.

Chris Rice   3

Squirrel Chase

Love taunts death,
Pursues in highest branches
And dares them to break.

Love flirts oblivious into trafficked street,
Provokes and dodges
Black tires spaced barely enough.

Love absorbs its object,
Unaware how closely death breathes
To one or both.
So preoccupied with the living,
Death has no say.
But is it love
Or only instinct of animal
If it knows not the fate of linear time?

For love increases when it learns its end.
And focused on its coming loss
Mixes love with grief;
So becomes stronger, yet not purer—
For though grief be not selfish,
It self involves.
Our paradox.

Ah, lovers, think not on it.
Preoccupy with the loving.

Chris Rice

I Aimed an Arrow Inward

I aimed an arrow inward
And let it fly.
It never struck a target,
Never reached a middle.
Shot from this borderland
It will forever fly—
Gain untold speed
Toward infinite inwardness.
There is an eternity inside me
Not of time or space,
Vast and perpetual.
But to contain what or whom?
I am too small to fill my fathomless self.

First Flake

Float into my field first flake of the year.
I write you, keep you now, and won't forget.
I wonder, too, if ever snow appeared
Without the hint of mother's sentiment—

Whose knee we sat and felt her coo delight
In tiny ears, and stitched our inner coats
With 'pure' and 'clean' and 'beautiful.' She
wrote
Her 'hmmm' and 'ooooh' and 'aw' on tiny
souls;

They clung like gath'ring flakes to blades of
green;
Soon melted, hid, and nourished in the
Spring.
Though fifty years have flown, yet resonate
When stills the sky and softly dusts with
white

My waiting hair. Snow, either word or sight,
Still conjures unremembered influence.
Forgot her lap, outgrew her knee with time,
But write these verses, hers as much as mine.

Chris Rice

Bread, Wine, and Water

I wish he had said it—
I can almost hear him—
Just after he pointed to the bread and wine
And gave them their reminding powers,
Might he have added
"Whenever you play in a creek,
Remember your baptism,
And that you are mine."

Tend

Your soul is a small patch of Eden,
In some ways, larger.
Take that spade over there
And plunge through your time-hardened soil,
Rake loose your rocks and sticks,
Pick through them and remove
Whatever you don't want anymore.
The weeds of your childhood
Are yours to keep
If you need excuses
(But you don't),
Or yours to rip up, roots and all,
And toss in the burn pile
To clear space for the new and the best.
Make room for sustenance,
Roots and berries,
Lettuces and curvy squash.
Beautify with blossoms,
Vines, stalks, petals,
Even a few thorns,
For they, too, have their beauty.
Delight in your surprise visitors,
Rodent brothers and winged sisters,
Ladybugs and inchworms,
Every silvery silken web spinner!
Pay attention to the seasons
Pray for sky's water,
Sun's warm, bright bath,

Chris Rice

And so remember it's not all your own doing.
Care. Care. Care.
Now, sit long hours in it.
Perfumed and nectar'd,
Brimming of color.
Sway its blooms with the breath of your
laughter.
Let tears lend their kaleidoscope sparkle to its
yellows and purples.
Stay. Stay. Stay.
Your soul is ever a garden.
It takes work.
Wonderful, wonderful work.

Crib

Grass points poke and tickle
My neck and back,
I'm wide-eyed in summer-warmed twilight,
As alone as I was in my cradle.
I send out two hands
Toward a zillion worlds that
Hover, tremble, and spin above
Like a mobile of toys just out of reach,
Strung this time by invisible lines—
Gravity.
We learn by trying to touch.
We grow by trying.

Chris Rice

Stages

We wake up center stage,
In History's middle—
Its very middle, we insist,
Because to each of us
The story self-writes for 'me.'

How soon the foggy question haunts our ears:
Am I to be a comedy or tragedy?
Not knowing which until it plays its end.
I cannot bear the wait!
I claim my title comic!

These others are my audience,
(Ha! They reckon me theirs! Imagine!)
Who exist not for themselves
But to applaud and weep for me.

Weep? I thought you said 'comic.'

Oh, comic it is!
Your tears are applause in disguise.
Your weeping is but my timely trick
To own you into my drama.
Having your tears, I have you,
And revel in my fresh-proven value.

Mark it—you soon will laugh
And wipe your wetted cheeks

Chris Rice   11

And shake your heads.
'He got us again!' you'll all exclaim
And clap your grateful hands toward me.
'Hooray for him! Comedy it is!'
And then I take another bow.

Ah, we all take frequent bows
And believe these others came to watch our
show.
But we, unnoticed,
Bow only to their round rumps,
For they too are bent, busy bowing to their
others!

We're all but Fools on wobbly stages.

Chris Rice

Dead Poets

How cliché.
On the day a poet dies,
They scan his works and words
For any thought of dying,
And upon its finding
Label it 'ironic.'

There is no special irony
In verse that mentions death.
For what poet, author, writer
Does not play near it? And often!

Death simply pokes around in every living
mind,
As does birth, love, nature, and brotherhood,
All tasty meats to nourish readers.

So sift through my piles of words
And find your jewel for any day!
But on that day I die
Do not strain for hidden hints
In lines I might have mentioned it
As if I'd penned them prophecy.
They are mere remarks
On one of living's plural parts,
Discovered on a happy day!

Quote for me another instead,

Chris Rice   13

Maybe Whitman, who sums his departure
thus:
"Look for me under your boot-soles."

His words will do just fine
Until that time
In bootless feet
We casually meet
On far more golden roads.

Chris Rice

Warm

If I were blind I still would know the sun,
But not the moon. It stabs this quiv'ring
heart!
To lose my moon, save only as a word?
Imagination, give her back as quick!
I gave her up for my poetic trick
But lost my way, and found me lunatic.

I Wear My Favorites Out

Even as I toddled half a century past,
I wore my favorites out.
Like my one shortest crayon,
And all my kindergarten pages
Doodled over in red.

I dump red sauce
Like lava over pasta!
And gorge until my belly hurts,
Tight as a playground kickball!
I hear its bouncy tune
Like I just kicked a home run.

A holiday tune barges uninvited into my head
And repeats and repeats all day, all Summer
day!
Silenced only and at last by sleep.
Please be gone by morning!

No less than a thousand mornings
I've passed along a single creek,
Kept tally of its hungry ducks
Who dive and kick their yellow clumsy webs
upside-down,
But lazy days they float and bump, or tuck
their heads and doze.

I doze on porches,
Sniff the scent of distant rain,

Chris Rice

Think it perfume, and hyperventilate!
Now awake and focused on new hurried
streams
That flush the curbside clean,
Till thunder is imperceptible,
And swept open is a tiny patch of blue.

In every blue winter night's horizon
I hunt the hunter Orion.
And make a deal of Venus
When she flirts like my best girl,
So obvious from the sky,
In plain sight of my envious Moon.

Ah, Lovely Moon, hide your jealousy.
You well know I nightly seek
Your circled face, your crescent smile,
And often spell you out in lyric!
One would think I just discovered you
And suffer Cupid's arrow prick!

Live to Be a Thousand

My infant self did not choose immaturity,
It was the natural state of things.
Sapling, pup, untried, innocent.
It's all a matter of timing.

Soon I learned to skip and giggle,
But also to whine and huff
And scrape my knees
Through witless schooldays.

Then came adolescence
And added pluck to dumbness.
I puffed out my skinny, hairless chest,
And rolled my eyes at the stupid world.
The happy miracle is this—
That any of us yet breathe
Beyond our adolescence!

Ah, what humor our early selves feed us now!
Now ripened and sturdy-built,
We laugh away how silly we were.

But what if I reach a thousand years?
Will I then look back
On these early-gray
Grown-up days,
And roll my eyes at
Today's confident half-knowledge?
Could I yet be so naive?

Chris Rice

Oh, I wish just one of us could live to be a
thousand
And shake the rest of us by our shoulders
And warn us how little we know.
But who of us would even listen?

We die too soon like gnats,
And pass down only penny-wisdom
To ones unable yet to grasp it.
Folly loiters these alleys,
Sloppy, slouchy, nonchalant,
Like a bully blocking our way.

At least with time our follies recede
(Though sadly leave room for newer ones).
Yes, years bring wisdom,
But I suspect fresh silliness too!

No one survives a thousand years
To smile and tell us what unfound fooleries
We might yet devise if given time.

Life is our perpetual punchline.
Laugh along.
Wisdom is in knowing our lack of it.

Curtains

Even our windows to the soul
Have their soft drapery.
When these eyes shut their last,
It's curtains of flesh on our final play
And this stage is forever empty.
Our children somehow know!
No wonder they crawl over our chests
While we doze on couches
And with tiny thumbs lift open these lids
To see if a soul is still in here
Or if playtime is ended.
No wonder they giggle
When these fringed velvets
Pop open wide
To meet their waiting eyes—
Their pudgy fingers have worked a miracle,
A resurrection!

Chris Rice

Kindergarten

It started in kindergarten
And now I yell at trees.

My early hand,
A quarter its current size,
Clenched twin pennies with tiny dates—
Nineteen-sixty-eight.

I smell sweaty copper in miniature palms,
Palms that could only escape half the distance
They now enjoy from my twice-grown and
whiskered face.

I daily traded two shiny cents for one waxy
carton,
So blue and so white.
The torn paper spout tickled my lips.
My throat gulped the cold thick milk.
I breathed hard between swallows,
My eyes darted the room from color to color.

That oatmeal cookie that took both fists to
hold?
Remember how it chewed.
I feel it on teeth that have since been lost.
(Rumor has it a fairy took them,
And left me coins!)

Look!

A box of fat crayons in rainbow order,
Big as clumsy branches,
Thicker than fingers.
I still smell them
In my mind's nose.
Bits of wax under tiny fingernails
From peeling paper off,
Fat tongue poking out to better the job.
Red is soon the shortest,
My favorite.

How do I hold these?
There is only one correct way?
That leaves me too many wrong ways!
Somebody teach me.

So began my inelegant crush on color.
I'm still in love, awkward love.
In fact, I yell at autumn trees,
Red and yellow,
When I drive past.
I don't know what else to do.
I can't contain myself.

Even today I had to look away
When yellow made eye contact.

Chris Rice

Rain

The air is gray, but not entirely.
There is a shimmering in the din
Of liquid coming back down.
A million fragile sounds
Join in slant for one deafening moment
And thrill my thirsty earth.
Every surface glosses, deepens,
And moves to lower places,
And the ground sops
Like brimming tears,
And the world weighs twice itself.

Who Has Summered at the Beach

Who has summered at the beach
And felt the push and roll of waves,
The trip and pull of undertow?

Who has floated the drift,
The sanded tide,
The back and forth,
The surrender and resistance
Of his body and will
To the omnipotent ocean?

Who has coped the sirens' lure
Toward bobbing in deep-float freedom
Against shore's solid promise of safety?

Who has dreaded the chomp
Of unseen sea monster,
Teeth through flesh,
Imagined or real, only inches away,
Twin-timed with adolescent delights
Of sparkle-splash,
Fizz and foam,
Sunny gasps,
Sky-tossed wet hair,
Salt lips,
Goose bumps,
Squint-blinking?

Who has then rested same humid night on his
pillow
Eyes heavy-shut and dark,
Exhausted from knockabout waves,
Still feeling them?

Then you know what the poet feels tonight
Trying to find his sleep,
Reeling
From today's rhythm and vowel.

Nostalgia

nostalgia: from Greek nostos 'return home' + algos
'pain.'

My age recounts his early days
(How can it be so long ago?)
That wished-for time, this happy ache,
This pleasure-pain, returning home.

Strong memory packed of grass and dirt,
Of forest creek, of wooden fence,
Of turning flips, of bikes and balls,
Uncov'ring snakes and arrowheads.

Of fishing lines on splintered piers,
Of body-surfing foamy waves,
Of stoking fires, pitching tents,
Of trekking mountains' ragged trails.

But long have rusted, rotted through
What I had hoped would always be.
So nature has her perfect way—
Her nature can't stop teaching me.

'm I wrong to miss my simple times?
The years roll on, their changes bring.
I'm sad my younger comrades find
Nostalgia over plastic things.

Chris Rice

Life Science

In that sleep before birth
I had no inkling,
Therefore I was not.
Good point, Descartes.

Then suddenly I was,
By a power not mine.

So now that I am aware,
Will I ever not be?
Good question, Hamlet.

And what beyond?
Good question, humankind.

I agree.
Resurrection is impossible.
But no more impossible than that *first* time I
came to life.

So I cannot rule out a resurrection.

Undertones

The jet's quiet, steady growl
Across the sky's near blackness
Carried in it the murmurs of a mother's voice
In a nearby room
Talking soft, lamplit nonsense
To her cooing child,
Delighting in his attention
While he stares into her
And flaps and kicks his limbs
And takes happy jerky breaths
In primitive glee
Hoping somehow to touch
Or lure her chatty smile even closer.
How I heard all that in a midnight jet
I'll never know.

Chris Rice

Neigh
(At Horseshoe Canyon)

Her shoulder twitches loose the damned fly
Without thinking 'damned.'
Her tail slaps another away
Without a thought.
She's done it a million times.
Another shiver of her rump
Agitates a dozen more
Which only swirl and settle again
Rearranged.
Who is more bothered, she or they?

Her brown globed eyes
Only ever show her bored or spooked.
What she might be thinking terrifies me—
Not so much what she thinks, but how—
In dumb mumblings
Like thick mud of mind
Unconnected to her meaty tongue.
Does she not know her language lack?
Does her tongue not ache to move?
To feel the glory of an L sound?
To bless, curse, thank, complain?

She seems content to drop her head,
Shake her mane,
And bite off a sun-warm bunch of clover.
Her teeth clop like hooves.
Maybe she's happy with this,

Chris Rice   29

Or maybe happy isn't a thing to her.
We can never know.

How I would miss my words.

Chris Rice

Fame Is an Africanized Bee

Oh, my dear Emily,
You left out the best part—
The honey!
That's not to say
Your poem isn't perfect.
But you also forgot
The worst part—
That they swarm
And almost kill you.

Lies

Same two hands
But smaller and chubby
Mashed shut these eyelids
And hid me from the scary world.

I pressed pink palms against tiny ears
Outshouted sounds I did not wish to hear
And like a magic trick, all disappeared.

Cotton covers tucked tight to my chin
Forged my nightly armor,
Assured me monster-proof.

And now,
Five decades flown,
I still fear what is only imagined.
And I yet try to magically unbelieve
Uncomfortable truth out of existence.

Outgrow your lies, boy.

Chris Rice

Hangover
(New Year's Morning 2013)

I woke before them all.
Not all, I say, but most,
Who slumber hard with faces down.
Who still half dream of yesterday
If at all they dream.

A feathered few rose before me
To splash in swollen creeks and preen;
A silhouette stag stared his motionless magic
From the foggy slope of a tree-spotted hill;
The sky in clumsy hangover
Dragged her gray gown along and scraped the
tired earth,
Darkened bark, deepened green,
Entangled slow and swirled in highest twigs
And misted them invisible,
Then revealed to me, then hid one ghosty
sycamore.
I gasped and laughed like a child at peeking
games.

I woke before them all.
I pictured billions on our spinning ball
In spectral skins, still too asleep to pray
To gods who've measured out another day for
them.
And so their gods must mortal wait like I do.
But only for a time.

Chris Rice   33

For the sun in its soon hour will nudge the
slumberers,
Evaporate the gray
And burn gold edges to the hills.
The world will squint and yawn,
And feel its stupor lift.

I woke before them all
To watch it happen—
To see them wake up one by one
To such happy news:
Another year is born.

Chris Rice

Exhausted Poet

Thoughts are swiftest.
Second, a wordless gesture.
Then speech, while I have breath to explain.
But to write? To write!
Even a fleet moment of my mind
Would waste an eternity in its writing out.
My mind is for only God and me,
(Though he knows it better).
With a word he made his universe.
But I—
I can scarce cough out my dust
Much less my universe.

On Time

Ah, first creature, first gift,
First command unrecorded:
Let there be Time!

Whether you are fabric, arrow, or wheel,
This we do know:
Without you there can be
No motion, change, or possibility.

Birth wakes us each to float your middle,
Our fathomless ocean with no horizon!
But we suspect you have your shores as we
have ours,
Unremembered and unforeseen.

Now you rob us of our begetters. Curse you!
Now you turn and give us heirs. Thank you.

Teary-eyed we stare you down
And fear you will annihilate us.
Then Albert dares us peek around you and
call your bluff!
You are not what you seem!
You call ours too, and taunt, for no one
surely knows.

We bend our minds to find your shape,
Have never met, and wonder what stuff you
are.

36   *Chris Rice*

Perhaps a frame for us?
Perhaps a clever gadget for your Maker
To veil himself above, behind?

Ah, if you have a Maker
Then you are not supreme!
For we have him too!
And his promise to outlast you!

So do your worst!
When you are gone we stand!
Eternity is not your measure
But your end!

Oh, Milton's self-devouring Time
You will run out your course.
What marker pass you now?
Have you reached your half?
Are you tired?

Chris Rice   37

Shy Poem

Please, don't read me out loud.
Just let my words roll in your quiet mind.
If you must share, silently point me out to
friends
And let them read me for themselves,
To hear me only in their inner voices.
Not with ears, not in stereo,
But in the centers of their heads.
What do I 'sound' like? Your own voice or
mine?
Can you feel the question mark going up?
Notice those imperceptible quivers and
tremors
Of tongue and throat
As if you were speaking.
But please don't speak aloud!
I would never move a molecule of air.
Rather let me run up and down your neurons,
Pleasantly fill up and drain your synapses.
Have my effect inaudible, invisible.
My only evidence this:
Your eyes skip in tiny darts across a page;
A corner of your lip turns up a bit;
Perhaps a gleam, a teary feel behind your
eyes
(Because you get me,
Not because you feel sorry for me).
Oh, don't feel sorry for me!
I'm truly happy.

Chris Rice

It's just that I'm shy, that's all.
I still want to be your friend.
I still want you to like me.
Do you?

The Language of Crows

This morning I understood
The language of crows.

From the back yard
An ink-black trio interrupted
Saturday's usual happy nature song
And scraped the innocent air
Like fingernails on chalkboards
With a hectic cacophony of squawking
So loud and so long
I almost wished for a moment of deafness—
Until my sudden waking brain translated!

I inhaled another cereal bite,
Dropped my spoon all clink and milky splash,
And rushed to the window.

Three, exactly three crows there were.
(I've heard they can count that high,
But they don't even know it's Saturday.)
And this was no pleasant gossipy gabfest.
They made no eye contact
Either with me or with each other.
They just hopped and bobbed
And coughed their ill-timed,
Unrhymed throaty caws
To the neighborhood entire,
Like three sirens
Warning and waking the world to danger.

Chris Rice

I was right!
A hawk perched stone-still on the iron gate,
Grim as hungry death,
Eyes blazing yellow
With obvious distaste for the blabby, tattle-
tale crows
Flapping inches away, making a deal of him.
He stared annoyed at an empty spot in the
sky,
His cover blown,
His breakfast now warned and vanished
Beneath the rose-hedge bower.
He'd have to wait a bit longer
For this morning's warm-bloody, bone-
crunchy morsel.

But how long?
However long it takes a crow to shut up
And a rodent to forget.

Soon enough she'll bumble back out
All furry and oblivious into the open clover
In search of her own morning delicacy,
Grub or beetle.

I went back to my cereal bowl
And dug my talons and beak
Into my helpless squealing prey—

Well, I scooped a spoonful of cereal

And slurped it up,
Chewed it to mushy bits,
And swallowed.

Chris Rice

No More

Fresh from the brothel,
Are we to be pitied or abhorred?
The pulpit says one, we hope for the other.
Do you forgive in the very instant?
Or is your reckoning equal to our conscience,
Which must wait for dark feelings to subside?
Caught in the act,
How long until "Neither do I condemn,"
Issues from your lips?
We answer in months, years, and lifetimes,
But you seemed eager in the moment
To jot in the dust
And dispel all accusers
At the drop of a stone.

I don't get you.
Yet in my deepest place
I want so badly
For you to be true.

To find my peace,
I'd rather be entirely wrong
And entirely forgiven,
Than devise some way
To disbelieve in one so like you.

Chris Rice   43

One-Piece Puzzles

An empty boat
Cups a soul
And hides a story.

A lone tree on a hill
Begs to shout her hundred-year secret.
Sadly, no steamy lung or trembling tongue
Have yet been wrought of wood.

A half-pair of gloves
Still as chilly death without its other half,
And how long since the last warm hand
within?

A single shoe
Haunts a roadside,
Most spooky if a child's.

I Was Larger When a Child

I was larger when a child
For then I contained
All of my possible selves!
My eyes were small then,
But wide open!
The world was mine!
My young lungs
Gasped at everything!
And gasping enlarged their capacity
To gasp at more!
I explored, sprinted, hopped,
Cartwheeled, climbed,
Twirled my brain dizzy,
Hollered, whistled,
Laughed with my whole shaky belly,
And never cared who heard or saw!

Most possible selves have since been
Shamed or scared away,
Chiseled off and swept aside.
Am I now left forever to this one
Shrunken version of myself?
Who convinced me to focus?
To tuck my head, blinders on,
And ignore the wide world?
To stop searching for new?
To maintain calm?
To fight off adrenalin?
To settle into a normal normal?

Chris Rice   45

I've grown-up.
I'm right-handed.
I know what I hate and like.
I live up to my nick names.
I leave my opinions unchallenged.
I've chosen sides once and for all.
I'm entrenched with only friends who agree.
I've declared my favorite color.
My accent is permanent.
My habits delineate my shape.
My labels choose my state.
My routines lead my way.

Wait! Wait!
Why should life be a funnel
To fewer paths, tighter doors,
Less risk, safe mistakes,
Less freedom?

Find reverse!
Undo these borders!
They constrict my chest, my neck, my mind.
I'm suffocating.
I don't want to be grown-up,
I want to be growing!

For of such is the kingdom.

Perfection

When we impose across our cityscapes
Unnatured gloss, neon signs,
Sharp, plumb, level lines,
Stacks and squares of darkened glass
Towering above grid-patterned streets
Restless with stilettos, stiff suits, lipsticks,
colognes,
Our frantic attention on glowing screens,
Comparing selves and others
To rectangled billboards of airbrushed
sexiness—
We have lost our way.

Beauty is in imperfection!
The slow-rise billow of the summer cloud;
The thoughtless meander of a creek;
The untamed roar of sudden rain;
The jagged chaos of a lightening streak;
The ailing leaf that dying, blushes red;
The splattered patch on a pinto's hide;
And the asymmetric spread of a dogwood.

Chris Rice   47

Rich Old Lady
(Making a Donation at the Goodwill Truck)

Her hair not silver but fool's gold
To match her shiny toy-like shoes,
The same phony hue,
Unnatural and stiff and oversized.
Her morning joints complained with cracks
and pops
As she forced them cold into her monotone
pantsuit,
Pressed and curveless as a slender plastic
doll's.
She tied and fluffed a gaudy scarf around her
pale neck
To throw its silent tantrum among all this
dullness.
There must be ruby lips to match!
She hunched and blinked at her mirror
While fingers trembled to aim bright lipstick
At its thin wrinkled target.
In a moment she declared herself 'done'
And turned to face her millionth, it seemed,
day.
Her attempt to undo aging
Rendered her no younger,
Just clownish,
With cakey makeup that mocks the
undertaker's.

She will sit at coffee today

　　　　　Chris Rice

With her gaggle of equally painted dames,
And giggle like they were young
—Only now with lower scratchy voices—
At this and all of Time's other effects:
That, yes, their teenage beauty has faded,
But thank God they aren't seventeen
anymore!
That their men are gone and missed,
But thank God they outlived their men!
That our makeup is hideous,
That it takes a lot more of it these days,
But someone please take our picture
And make sure our undertakers render us just
this way
In case our caskets are to be open!
They laugh and stir and sip,
Saucers rattle, spoons clink against coffee
cups,
With crimson lip marks on their porcelain
edges
As one, then another,
Hold all happy sparkly eyes
To retell one of this week's funny moments
Or some long forgotten memory
And how it's not so bad to age
And they all nod, and stir
And each of them glances discreet
With a bit of longing
At perfectly curved, unwrinkled young
models
Smiling toward them

Chris Rice   49

From covers of magazines
On the rack behind her fool's gold hair.

Chris Rice

Then Sings My Soul

My palm pressed hard against the rock
And level with the pounding at my chest,
I lean in, gaze up and find its height.

It hasn't budged a thousand years
Though rain has scrubbed but tiny layers
And offers fingers just enough
To find and fight and ache and strain.

Not to defy our tyrant gravity
But use it, and cooperate,
And turn this work to play.

I tap that urge in all mankind
To cool our lung up closer to our sky
But lacking wings make use of other gifts
(If God had meant for us to climb
He would have shaped us arms and legs…
…oh!)

Like lover's breath tingles the neck
The whitened sun and empty blue combine
above,
Both warm and chill my naked skin,
Seduce me up and in.

My head rocked back,
My focused eyes,
I suck one deep-nostrilled breath,

Chris Rice 51

Nod to assure myself,
Commit my body entire
(One cannot partly go)
Then in a single motion
Separate it from the ground below.

Up now, and up,
Words and thoughts evaporate.
What burdens fall away!
Sensation takes the lead,
And hands and eyes and feet
Decide without words
What to trust,
What to skip,
Rarely more focused,
Never more alive.

And work and rest,
Not rivals but brothers,
Take their turns
And in their time
Deliver me breathless to my summit.

And only then
Resurrects a line
From childhood hymnody
And whispers sturdy words and melody
Through muscle, gut and mind.
The tune is in the wind,
The truth is in the rock.
I see much farther than my six-foot self.

Chris Rice

Then sings my soul.

Cool tears that somehow reached my jaw
unnoticed
Cling there, tickle, break free and fall,
Such tiny drops for massive gratefulness,
And stain the dirt a hundred feet below
Where lone I stood just histories ago.

What to Do with Guilt

For God's sake, don't drown in it!
Greet it with a firm handshake
And unflinching eyes,
Tears and all.
Do not pretend it isn't there—
Even so, it crushes.
Put to use its persistence.
Change its name to 'conscience,'
Weed out others' superstitions,
And drown instead in mercy.

Chris Rice

First Memory

Low light hums dim
In the night room.
I hold smooth white bars
And stand to the crib
To peer inside.
I cannot see him.
Try your tiptoes.
I push one hand between the bars
To a scratchy blanket
With a red stripe and a yellow one
But colors don't have names yet.
I feel the dark.
I hear him breathe.
What is he?

A Lost Art

We always know where Pop is.
We can hear him whistle
From anywhere in the house.
Never a whole song,
Just the first few lines
Over and over.
It sounds him ever happy!
It's a lost art.

I've never asked him
If he remembers learning how.
Being a score years closer
To that day than he,
I don't remember either.

What I do recall
Are childhood songs
That taught me
Whistling proves me brave,
And lightens the burden of hard work.

How we seasoned experts
Love to teach our kids the craft!
That eager apprentice
Fixed on our mouths,
Imitating, adjusting, trying over and over!
How serious her concentration,
The pink wet pucker,
The hyperventilate blowing,

Hoping for a different sound this time.

And when it happens at last
Her eyes pop wide!
Her jaw drops!
The room is inhaled!
The pucker returns in an instant
To make sure it wasn't a fluke!
Hurry! Hurry! Hurry!
Show everybody what I can do!
How we all make merry
Like she just won the world!

Is it the unremembered elation
Of this one childhood moment
That returns every time we whistle?
Why whistling still makes us happy
Decades and decades later?

Perhaps the true art is not the whistling
But the being happy.
Pop gets it.

Chris Rice   57

Sky, the Word

I

Sky, the word, is too, too small.
What word can ever say it all?
It tilts our mind toward cliché,
Reduces sky to blue or gray.
Three spiky letters scratch him true,
And kindergarten paints him blue,
Thus trained to oversimplify,
The babe, the sage, all, mumble 'sky.'

To shape his name with tongue and teeth,
One syllable, one borrowed breath,
He lends himself whose name we shout—
Chest draws him in, and breathes him out.
We scarcely give a glance his way
Unless he darkens middle-day,
When to the sky our face reflects
To scan the cloud, to weigh its threats

Of thunderbolt, of whirling wind,
Whose terrifying beauty spins
Like dance, but to obliterate.
And pregnant clouds precipitate.
Come flakes and sleet and slanted rains!
Our local maps you rearrange!
You level life and leave it strange,
Then clearing, azure, soothing, change.

Chris Rice

So sky, that word, that childhood friend,
May span beyond its simple trend,
And swirl the blue, the storm, the air—
Ah, this is but the thinnest layer!

II

Space, the word, expanding now
Includes the night, the stars, and how
Our senses stretch, become aware—
"Tonight the moon is over there."
But moon and stars expose our lack—
Still night is "black," and 'black,' and black.
And 'space' and 'sky' yet render blind
And veil immensities behind.

Whose life-years ever last enough
For light-years to convey their stuff?
Of anti-stuff, Orion's toys,
Of comet tails and asteroids,
Of dwarfing star and galaxy,
Of blackest hole and entropy,
Where hottest blaze meets chillest cold,
All spinning specks in mixing bowl.

Now scrambled to our highest roofs,
We train the lens and rummage proofs
That space is full, yet mostly bare
(Though gods are sometimes rumored there).
Come journeyed from its burning source,
A hint of light now strikes our porch

Chris Rice   59

And boasts the edge of all we know!
We've reached where we can never go.

Yet still we settle for the word,
And keep it small, and said, and heard;
Concede our tick in Time and Size
And let the letters summarize.
We whisper, "Other worlds might be."
We've seen what we will never see.
We lose ourselves, we find our place,
We hold our mouths, and call it 'space.'

Chris Rice

Psalm Eighty-Eight-and-a-Half

Like being stabbed without a dagger
Nor anyone wielding it
(Having one to blame does not help anyway),
It all aches.
My instinct is to clutch where it hurts,
But I cannot find where.
How long have I run or stumbled,
Crawled or collapsed?
It's all the same.
Breathing asks too much of me.
When is it done?
I whisper the question just to hear someone!
What is the cost?
More blood than fills my veins,
More loss than my lifetime's store,
More tears than should be wrung from any
eyes.
Will I ever hope again?
I've heard it said,
Though hardly believe it,
'Enduring builds endurance.'
Prove it.

December 12

Wrap tight your sweater, closer still,
'Gainst flakes who tumble on the wind.
The poet lent them each a soul
And marvels at their journey down.
Whispered farewell to fath'ring cloud,
All sisters, brothers, hurried flew,
Their race to find where each may land
But slowed by barely lighter air.
A roof, a rose, their destiny
Perhaps to tickle window's pane
Or, so delights the spying lass,
Black paper 'neath her looking glass.
All swirl and settle, purpose done—
Unless pink hands scoop up and press
And hurl at unsuspecting friend!
(O, double purposed, lucky ones!)
Be only brief your frozen rest.
Be slushy soon, and soak the soil.
So melt with spring, aid well its bloom,
Evaporate and chase your sun.
Now circle up into your skies,
Your glory both to fall, to rise!
Upgathered mist, becloud the night,
Fall back to me, new, soft, and white.

Chris Rice

Do Not Write Me Larger Than I Am

Do not write me larger than I am.
Do not write me more interesting, more
flawed, more saint.
Why conjure hero where none stands?
Why this appetite for elegy?
Why dig for scrap and artifact?
Why sneak to peek behind a non-existent
curtain, as if we are very different?

Surround me not in your mind with objects
rare, nor trinkets exotic.
Don't trick me out, don't decorate me to your
liking.
Nor pity me in your projected suffering,
For I do not writhe in tormented days.
I do not eke my words from passions or
pains.
Nor revel I in wantonness, altered state,
sedative
(The saddest fiction about 'all fictionists').

True, I have a gift to toy with words, but that
is all—
A story, a song, a game.
Nothing to decipher.
No tortured artist.
No secret life.
No mystery.
I'm shrouded up in normalcy.

Chris Rice 63

I am not 'called,' 'anointed,' 'blessed.'
I look for God no more than most;
I hear from him far less.
(Term it religion if you will, or superstition,
crutch.
I argue not, I simply trust I'm pardoned from
a cross.)

My summary this:
I like my coffee, beer, creeks and trees.
I social best in twos and threes.
I share my moonlit porch with friends.
I dust, cycle, shower, shave,
Mow my lawn, climb big rocks,
Do push-ups, eat burgers,
Watch the news, sleep.

So if you must write me, write me ordinary.
Better, do not write me down at all.
See here—
I've done it for you.

Chris Rice

Slow Explosion

If time could lapse before my eyes
I'd stare through autumn's weeks
At but one tree
Whose slow explosion
Would surprise and thrill me
Like a firework!

Edges

I found my life on the edge of seasons
Where runs a childish game of give and take.
Yes, you're invited Boy! Jump up and play—
More often, find these cycles playing you.

One morning gray is peaceful, happy, light.
The next is heavy, aches its dullness in.
I hear damp rain and sleep a day away
Or rebel-rise and charge out with a grin!

I groan the puddle step that drowns my shoe,
Then revel in such fortunate surprise!
A thunder clap first strikes my heart with
dread
Then thrills my gut, wild jitter laughs inside!

Cool breezes tingle bumps onto my arms,
Caress my soul, expand my empty lungs.
Then shoulders hunch, complain against this
cold.
Same coldness stings my nostrils, wakes new
life.

Today I choose to hide, tonight I'll seek.
For now the pupil's role, tomorrow teach.
Sometimes I raid, at times I must defend.
Now celebrate, now weep with those who
weep.

Chris Rice

I lug my mood and lend it to the Moon,
Or find one there and call it to myself,
Hear how she coaxes howls from lonesome
wolves,
Or shines our double smile—the Sun's and
mine!

Same fiery Sun that blinds and causes squint,
Yet warms the Globe and dapples tree-lined
yards!
Though 'all the world's a stage,' mere half is
lit
While other half sleeps under twinkling stars.

For circling 'round our sphere, two edges play
And chase as if the twain shall ever meet!
Sunrise, you chase in vain your Sunset fair—
She, equidistant, ever chases you!

Both constant running from, and running to!
And from your hopeless circles spring our
life!
A suited prooftext for this tale I count—
That borders are the place for paradox;

That paradox is pump that moves us all;
All tensions beg release, first fly then fall!
So blurs the edge where dance the light and
dark,
Where exclamation point taunts question
mark.

Chris Rice   67

And so I teeter-tot on seasons' rims
And balance 'tween a thousand tug-o-wars
And half-sleep, half-awake in morning's hope
And trust in dusk's sweet promise—coming
rest.

Both full and empty, energized and still,
Connected yet alone in vacuumed space,
The coin's two sides, like Providence and
Will,
Not opposites, but all to be embraced.

Embraced! Our wax and wane! Our ocean
tides!
And here on seasons' edges find our lives.

Chris Rice

Grace

Ah, silly children!
Toss away your measuring sticks
And play.

Only immeasurable things matter,
And they have already been
Reckoned.

The measure is held up against Another
And by no mistake,
You are the ones declared worthy.

Our Best Minds

Are the world's best minds in our past?
Historic, still, dead and buried?
Turning with the earth in silent graves?
The mighty hymns and sonnets
That ring deep and true
Leave us lamenting, too,
For such writers write no more.
We now settle for celebrities
And pay them to strum their strings,
To don their glitter,
To be our prophets,
To speak for God.
We pay them for it.
We pay them for it!
They tickle our itching ears
And offer us goosebumps and candy—
Exactly what we throw our tantrums for,
What we demand our mommies buy for us
From child's-eye-level choices
At the checkout line.
Grow up!
They mimic, but they are not the thing!
Fading plastic flowers with no aroma.
Away with the noise of your songs
And nursery rhymes!
It's time to rise and do the difficult work!
Tend the Garden!
The world starves for writers again!
For great minds to appear!

Chris Rice

Ah, let there be just one!
Who will it be?
Where are you now?
In a womb?
At your elementary desk?
Waiting out a few more generations?
Withering unknown on your dying bed
Because you were afraid to risk?

Clues

We think of times outside our own.
We feel unfairness in our guts.
We ache for renewal.
We despise decay's stench.
We shake a fist at death.
We tremble at its threat.
We fight to heal.
We long for love.
We own a word for 'mystery.'
We want to be our better selves.
We explore inside our souls and out.
We seek out beauty and crave its name.
We dot our yards with bits of Eden.

Optimist

Should that rainbow crack,
Collapse to earth,
Who would count the multitude
Of bugs and men
Smashed by the sheer weight of indigo?
Who would report, and to whom?

Should that cloud unravel,
What confusion for passers-by gazing
upward,
Death-gripping strangers-lovers' arms!
Lovers who can't save.
Yet lucky,
Both for having lovers,
And that unraveled clouds do no harm
Though they blacken the sun.

Why such panic breaths
And instant watery sockets?
Is it for want of understanding?
Are we not always mere seconds from
understanding?

Hey, white hot sun? Dead dry moon?
Is it you who keep us green and wet?
You who pedal our cycles in life-gift
constancy?
Would you hear us if we thanked you—
You who tilt our spin, and shove us around,

Chris Rice   73

Like bullies mocking shy girls at the dance
hall?
Until, of course, the music stops.
All new silence dizzies us.

But—
Crack and unravel, you sky!
Shake, you ground! Rattle us queasy.
Blur, you stars! Sting our eyes.
Your terrifying speed yet looks still from here.
And I will believe my eyes.

Somehow all things hold together.

Chris Rice

Pillow Math

Rude morning dawns; I lie here half-awake
And moan for doubled sleep before this day.

I'm back to bed too soon, and wishing sleep
Were but the tenth (and not the third) of life.

Chris Rice 75

River Talk
(On A Walking Bridge Above Foster Falls)

I stopped and overheard the river talk
And saw its silver slipping through the rocks
Which torture gladness into liquid's need,
Now pile it up, now press it into speed.

Whose drops, first lonesome molecules,
adhere
And gather to a path which least resists;
Collect from caves and springs and rivulets,
From crusted bark made dark by morning
mists.

Assembled for no purpose of their own
And knowing not, yet doing all they know,
Haste to adventures, quick and white and
loud,
Or nudged aside to swirl in silent pools.

How soon clear current sucks them back
again
To join the flow of fellow worshippers—
Yea, worshippers I say, for sounding praises
While humbling, down and down, to lower
places.

Their burbled voices, happy hollow moans,
Each trickle like a whispered joke for all,
For all erupt in laughter as they fall,

Chris Rice

Not far, but inching, inching toward the sea.

Why now their joy, existing to obey
Kind gravity, their single-minded tyrant
Ever pushing down? Consider this:
He gives his orders in obedience

To his Creator too. The mover and the moved
Both gladly serve the Same, as do we all.
Though not so gladly, we who have our wills.
And so we learn by watching water fall.

Some drops will roll their way to ocean floor,
The steady journey of a hundred years.
Some part today and rise toward our Star,
Bid farewell to this momentary mix.

I'm happy to have mingled too today,
At least to stand above as eavesdropper,
To overhear the self-free praise they offer
And feel it swell inside my silent self.

Chris Rice   77

Painter's Tantrum

Like an exasperated child
I roll my eyes
With tortured sighs
Toss back my head
And complain to God,
"Can we please have a new color?!"

Chris Rice

You Cannot Prove

You cannot prove
That I go nowhere
When I sleep.
Like every child who milk-drunken yawns
And strains to keep her eyes as wide
As windows open to this wonderful world
But can't resist the warm drowsy lure
Of the other side
And so they shut,
I too slip away
And leave a whole body behind
Still breathing
To assure you, not me.
For I am happily gone for a while
Unless you nudge and call
And pry my windows open.
Is this why we say "go" to sleep?
Because we travel to such familiar, such
strange
Destinies?
Every morning brings me back, so far.
The sun, the birds, sing me awake again
And land me on my feet
And let me smile for just a few more minutes
While those still fresh dreams dissolve
As quickly as the blankets cool
Without my body's heat.
I want to go back.
But days will always interrupt

Chris Rice   79

And have their own stuff to smile about.
Life's a teeter-totter ride between the two,
Day, night, day, night, day, night.
So shut my grateful lids tonight,
And coax me once again
To a heaven or a similar place.
You may not believe.
But you cannot prove
That I go nowhere
When I sleep.

Unexplainable

Language is a lovely mystery!
We have a word
For wordless things!
Which betrays this in us—
That we suspect our lack.
So we have assembled a needle
That points us in impossible directions
And spins our compass wild and dizzy.
We thus admit
There might exist
Thoughts and Things
Too big for us.
In the meantime
Let's shrug,
And call them what they are,
Unexplainable.

Waves

Drawn to the shore again and shoeless,
I'm poured a potent drink of equal parts
Terror and amusement.

Bubbles hiss at my heels
And pull me forward in foamy swirls
Like tiny mimic storms.

Water walls crash in rows before me!
Their repetition works a spell
And slacks my mindless jaw open.

Time after time
This ocean heaves and rushes toward,
Intent to drag me out.

I stand my ground,
Ever-shifting sanded ground,
Which grain by grain abandons me
Till I subtle sink,
But an inch.
A mere inch!
Is this your worst, you thunderous curls?

Were there no eye to observe you
Still you would move and move and move.
What thought! I am exhausted!

What fearful weight of water sucked to earth

Chris Rice

And nudged around by the Moon!
Within, I dread such primal heaviness;
Without, enjoy these cold-tickled shins.

Did I just mention the Moon
Who nightly casts her selfless light to this
lucky surface?
Ungrateful ocean! You shatter her so quick
And toss her back to the sky in pieces!

But look there, beyond!
Gray meets gray in slightest curve
So blur and far away
It might as well be eternity.

I kneel in rippled shallows,
And bare my chest to haughty waves
And dare them, or dare perhaps myself.
They neither blink nor flinch.
I can't undo a single one.
And therein is my place.

Before this ocean
I am diminished without remedy, save this:
I will rise and play—yes, play!
And saw the salty air thus, with mighty
gestures
And make my loud decrees to the deaf and
deafening sea—

Carry on your ceaselessness!

Chris Rice   83

Slow not your millennial rhythms!
Never tire, nor complain!
Come again!
Come again!
Come again!
And wash the sand!
And wash the sand!
And wash the sand!

Chris Rice

The Poet Interrupts

The poet interrupts my Now
With other worlds and times
And rapid floods this desert soul
With passions never mine.
When Yeats intrudes with bee-loud glade,
Or Whitman's sobbing bells,
I spy a word on handwrit page
And own that sound it tells.

But dare I call it owning
If the episode's not mine?
Or is it mine in truer sense,
A rarer glimpse behind?
What lyric tool, what poet's trick!
A word's a lens for 'seeing,'
For I am bid inside of it,
Now it's inside my being!

I feel a tumbling in the gut,
My blood and breath both startle.
Warm, briny tears are piling up,
And blur the words, and sparkle.
Such panoramas 'hind these eyes
(These eyes should never see)
Are seen and heard and felt, and taste
Like sobbing in a dream.

If glimmer could a feeling be,
If heartache made a sound,

Chris Rice

If loving were a scent instead
Where angels fly around,
Then poet, chase these holy ghosts
To wrest their secrets from them
And leave them panting with surprise
A mortal's overcome them.

Then like a hero hasten home
Come, wing back to this age,
And spread them out, your golden spoils,
On naught but ink and page!
Astonish me at jeweled thought!
At words ne'er thought combined!
At longed-for news from distant realm!
And so, from distant time!

For past is there, tho' memory's gone
By single draft of Lethe,
And future may or may not come
Yet still I choose the breathing.
And still I choose the reading, too,
Still blame you, poet, for it!
I dream awake at your command.
Unlock my soul. Restore it.

Chris Rice

Words

A word spoken
Is but warm vapor
That cools and dissipates
In little time.

But ink survives breath,
So use with care
Your pens and keystrokes.
The words you write outlive you.

Chris Rice

Impossibility Theory

I cannot decide which is more impossible,
Life or death.

If we, as we are told,
Begin to die the moment we are born
Then life is the miracle,
Enduring against the odds,
Forcing its fragile illogical self into
A universe rigged to wind down.

The grief and anger at a life lost
Point us to our inward rebellion
Against omnivorous death—
That woven into unlikely awareness
Is the notion that death should not be,
That death is the ruiner,
Not the norm.

Consider.
If nothing else takes us,
We die of natural causes.
But did we also rise to life naturally?
Or do we each arrive improbably, impossibly?

I have the same battle
With other energies and lacks—
Light and dark,
Heat and cold.
With other unattractive opposites—

Chris Rice

Order and chaos,
Matter and vacuum,
Never and forever.

All is one staggering miracle.
Every galaxy,
Every electron,
Every warm lung.

And here is my theory—
Everything is impossible!
It would require omnipotence
To make any of this happen.

Chris Rice

Starlings

Crowded starlings pick clean the yard.
One startles now, and all they fly,
Then whir and settle back again.
They followed never knowing why.

Now do they own familiar friends?
Or do they nameless flitting go
To hold their place in multitude,
Yet never known, and never know?

Have eyes to meet with others' eyes?
Or bound to scan but dirt and skies?
Is all but breath and sleep and food?
Such noises made! But understood?

Be more than noise! Please be a song!
Be more than unconnected throng
Of soulless chemistries and fates!
Please, be it Love perpetuates!

Ah, Love compel! 'The Love that moves'
Not feathered ones, but readers! You
Who populate cold crowded streets
In overlapped peripheries.

Chris Rice

My Devils Sing

My devils sing it thus:
"Friend, if you desire it, then it must be.
Restraint will bring you only harm.
Let go the shackles of laws and conscience
And be free.
See how we Defend you?
Look now how your angels Accuse!"

My angels sing their silver answer:
"Friend, you need neither defense nor
accusation,
But Pardon."

Today I side with my angels.

Chris Rice   91

Dying Alone

He asked the earless air
As if it already agreed:
'What is worse than dying alone?'
Within me whispered a surprise reply—
Worse than dying alone
Is dying famous.

For who can be fairly summed
In an afternoon of strangers' elegies?
Their stories, manufactured
And fastened to your name with tears,
Though surely kind, are slanders.
Untrue. Not you.
They'll dab their eyes,
Embrace in some felt need for you,
Echo your name around high-vaulted rooms,
And lament one who truly never was,
One projected for themselves,
One for whom your name was borrowed.
You saw them do it while you lived.
They will continue when you die.

But I say let them!
For they will also smile
And in your borrowed name
Find at least a reason to gather,
And gathering is good for us.
Take heart in this, man:
In that afternoon

Chris Rice

A crowded room
No longer suffocates you,
You no longer need its breath.
Your ears are shut to their voices,
Your lips motionless and disinterested to
clarify or defend,
Your mind at final peace.

Waste no thought on their false versions.
They speak not of you, but of their better
imaginings of you.
Let them have them.
Fret not today, while you yet breathe.
Think not on how you will be thought,
Or what you will leave.
Those friends you truly know
Will smile and weep
In proper proportion
In their inner cathedrals.

Still your mind and pulse right now, dear sir,
as you will then.
Employ instead today's energies to this living!
Simply be.
And let the rest be rest,
When worms will sort and redisperse your
elements
And your angels do their equal duty
With your soul.

Chris Rice

Borrowed

Quite unaware those ancestors beneath
The grass I crawled on chubbied infant knees.
All given back, renewed like babies' teeth
With clover sweet and pollened by the bees.

My lung has warmed her air, her wing to
soar,
And now her birdsongs play my soul out
loud.
And life itself not mine but borrowed ore,
And maybe soon my drink that thundercloud.

My breath has filled yon chest before this day
On cotton row, in woods where boys once
played,
Or (steals my breath a moment to survey)
'Haps on a Savior's cross a world away!

He loans his mountain peak, his rippled
shore.
If owning all I could not love it more.

Chris Rice

Hoarder

I can barely crawl
Through my soul's living room
Today.

I swear I'm no hoarder.
This was all dumped on me
Unawares.

These messy heaps
Floor to roof
Of unseen eternal treasures
Leave me stunned
Breathless
Tearful
Grateful.

Chris Rice   95

I Was Just Thinking

I was just thinking
And every thought
In shapes of words
Poured its flood of impulse to my tongue,
Quivering ready
To form and say aloud.
But there's a constraint kept my tongue idle,
Like bit and bridle under tender-taut reins
(Unless one choose to set it loose
Or let it slip while sleeping.)
So every thought
In shapes of words
Remained inside my God-jolleyed skull
To keep it close where only he and I could
hear.

First
How lonesome it would be without him
there.
Second
How clamorous
If sat we all untamed
And chirped our incessant chaoses,
Whatever sparked inside these heads of ours.
Third and Fourth
There's noise enough inside this one, and…
How kind of God to stay and listen.

Chris Rice

Adorned

I saw you stand and pointing down,
Your sidewalk paved, your polished shoe,
Your lawn boy trimmed your green for you,
And chemist killed your holy ground.

You shamed my lawn unmanicured,
"It speaks you lazy, careless, odd;
We owe to neighbor, self, and God
To tend and care and cultivate!"

Come, heap your vain theologies!
Still I recline on soiled knees
To gaze and gaze on handiworks,
To praise and praise and praise their worth!

Bright dandelions—yellow smiles!
A sea of violets never sown!
So who's to judge what's overgrown?
What's ugly weed? What sores the eyes?

Look! Truer life has found its day,
Erupted through this phony turf!
Reminding how our life on earth
More beauty finds in wilder ways!

Red berries dot my carpet green,
Sweet curly pea vines reach for suns,
White clover perfumes float the wind,
Uninterrupted glory runs!

Chris Rice   97

For I recall Divinest Son
Who juxtaposed in words to warn:
The lilies of the field adorned
And jealous cloak of Solomon.

So tend your lawns as I tend mine
But leave enough for chance and grace
To set their seeds and vie for space
And fill the crevice with surprise.

Chris Rice

Oak in October

On my chilly Thursday ramble,
Clouded gray but not entirely dark,
I near an autumn tree and feel her undertow.
The whole atmosphere beneath hums her
yellow.
The close air shimmers bright and pulses
almost warm
And wafts out in even wider waves
And covers me complete, and draws me in,
And spreads the glow of her gilded dress
Through my windows and into me.

My skin borrows her light, now twice lent.

Her leaves! Some have spun and drifted down
To overspread the ground at her feet,
Wet and heavy like a golden snowfall.

I tread with caution.

Her soaked and darkened bark, almost black
(The only contradiction to her yellow blaze)
Begs a touch by more than eyes.

She aches in stillness,
Smoldering yellow melancholic joy
For someone strode past her today and
noticed her!
And neither of us knows what to do next.

Chris Rice   99

I glance away out toward the cool gray
And take a panic step toward its sanity.
But we both know I will turn again,
And so I do, and so I find her sad smile.

"Tomorrow I return," I comfort.

"Tomorrow I change," she laments.

"So I will write you down and keep you!"

"But how," she calls, "am I to keep you?"

Chris Rice

Doubter's Prayer

You knew we'd come to this!
You let us anyway?

Why would you allow
(Allow, I say, to nod your sovereignty)
Allow us rank our minds superior?
To figure you out, to cast you aside
With temporary caged thoughts
That rattle our pre-cracked, pre-rotting skulls?
(For every skull that ever hummed a thought
before
Is empty now.)

Are we innocent or arrogant
To think our tiny thoughts so high?

Do you allow us such bold approach?
Such inquiry into your motive?
(Oh, motive, please be love!)
Seal we our doom by asking if you're even
there?
Or is your grace enough for even this?

Comes a time when we will
Know as we are known?
When question marks collapse in small,
explosive puffs of dust?
Their dry and powdered ink settles,
Your kind finger presses through

Chris Rice   101

And writes the answers plain for us?

Ah, speed that day!
And in our meantime tickle us with faith
And give us brothers to remind,
And together shoulder such dizzying loads
As knowing self and finding you.

Chris Rice

Hindsight

Even as a youngster I wondered—

How windswept autumn leaves resembled
acrobats;

How the sky used colors, not words, to brag
uninterruptedly;

How the red-haired girl's hair was not red;

How incomplete was a stick figure;

How clouds were rarely white, but cream and
gray and purplish;

How a coffee ring was round like the sun;

How a breeze spread chills across my arms
even as the sun warmed them;

How satisfying was the sound of a stone
dropped in the deepest part of the creek;

How the distance always looked a little hazy.

There was no way for me not to end up
Poet or painter.

Chris Rice   103

Birthday

So blessed today my grateful knee to bend.
Blessed! All these earthen trips around the
sun
Since lung first filled inside my golden friend,
And to the year exactly twenty-one!

He wriggled, blinked, all perfect, pink, and
bare,
Then kicked small legs, his fingers curled, and
toes,
Outstretched new arms to feel the welcoming
air.
Today into what sturdy man he grows!

I knew him not those twenty years he grew,
But felt no lack, no slow dissolve of Time.
Yet now I wonder how I never knew,
Or how in shortest days this friend is mine!

I had no inkling on that happy day
(No thought of future comrade stirred within)
That in Divinest Heart a plan was made
Before our empty world began to spin:

From Adam forth a globe would populate
And billions crowd his mountains, plains and
hills,
And all would intermingle fortunes, fates;

And all would try their strengths, and test
their wills.

Though none self-choose to be or not to be,
And none self-choose the hour, nor the
street—
It's Providence decides first day we cry!
So Providence decides which ones we meet.

And Providence has surely blessed Himself
And plots the steps of two unlikely sons.
My life spills over now our days are crossed,
And brother next to golden brother runs.

Chris Rice

105

To Sun, Moon, and Men

I disobeyed my father's frequent warnings,
And often dared you blind your awe-filled
son!
My child-self squinted at your perfect edge
And to my memory burned your razored
roundness.
Thank God these eyes survived their
innocence,
And found me luckier than Icarus!
Since then, ten thousand times you've sped
my sky,
No longer gaze direct, outgrew audacity.
Blaze on, Fair Sun, kind ruler my days,
And pulse your fire to blush my waiting face;
For had this man no eyes I'd know you still
From heat, not light, all sourced inside
yourself!

Now, crisp and cratered Moon, you lend light
too;
Reflection is a sort of borrowed light,
Yet only light—no heat's inside of you.
How soft your silver rays and shadows cast,
Twice lent your light when last it reaches us
Or thrice, reflected in another's eyes.
But there's no source inside your dusty self,
No pow'r to dry our seas or forge us clouds.
Kind warmth is not the gift you bring our
nights,

Chris Rice

But with another comfort ease our minds.
For spying you, we know our hiding Sun
Still shines! And one last thing of you Sweet
Moon—
Though weaker, lesser orb, in this way better:
At you we get to stare and stare and stare!

Now Mortal, what are you? What sort your
light?
A lifeless surface only to reflect?
No! Inner power blazes 'neath your skin!
Consuming King and Kingdom roar within!
Please, do your passive work like glowing
Moon,
But radiate your inward Kingdom too!

The News

Over and over
Tell your kid he is a failure
And he is bound to become it.

All day long
Broadcast to your societies
Only the worst that humans do to each other
And they will live up to it.

Our smug, obsessed, self-appointed experts
Smirk at us from cold lit boxes,
Predict our dooms,
Paint demons of our brothers,
Stoke our fears, blame the others.

A carefully chosen fraction of truth is a lie.
Do not believe the distorted funhouse mirror
They hold up to our faces.

We are more than this.

Chris Rice

The Feel of Words

Words are like wapled voisties.
They can habble the cuviest of dacklers.
Have you ever noticed how wingly
Are all the turlations we boffle every day?

Even nonsense has a soundy significance,
A jepitudinal heft, if you will.
Within every bursky remark
Lurks at least one pounce-wound jepitude.

So be watchful, fellow ombellivors!
Much of their meaning
Is tucked inside their soundiness.
Words don't just say,
They feel.

And every word with meaning now,
Started out gibberish.

Chris Rice   109

Too Much I Love
(A Hymn)

Too much I love this world you made!
Her colors sting like death,
Her shapes and movements drown my heart,
Her beauties halt my breath!
Her music, vistas, flavors, smells,
My frailties overrun!
I often swoon when shines her moon
Nor dare outstare her sun!

I live on brinks of sweet-sickness—
Too much a boy should bear!
If rumored heaven betters this,
I beg for new eyes there!
New ears to listen; more supple tongue
To mimic holy tunes;
And simpler nose to fill my lung
With long forgot perfumes!

But should you choose to change me not
Please offer mercy's cover,
Else I should die where death is not
And spoil New Eden's lovers!
Too much I love this world you made,
She echoes better places,
And homesicks me till we shall see
Direct, with unveiled faces.

Chris Rice

Soul

In a broth of brainish chemistry
Do a man's thoughts romp and splash,
But he is far more than this.
His radius, mid-chest to fingertip,
Cannot confine his reach or embrace.
His muscle and sinew will never portray how
truly strong.
His booming voice unfit to shout him loud
enough.
His thumping heart scoffs at bordered maps,
Flies to lovers far, reaches heaven.
His dreams carry him wild and anywhere
While the bed cradles mild his cranium.
His fleshy vessel sails—no—floods oceans
outward from himself
To seek, to include, to affect.
His desire could surely burn to ash
More forested worlds than ours.
His time spans untold years
(If time or years be even the measure)
Beyond his birth and passing.

This skin is just a skin,
A metaphor for itself.
I am not contained by my so-called edges.

Chris Rice   111

Just Kids

Those crayon marks
On your nursery wall
Were simply practice.

We are all just kids
Still compelled to scratch a mark on this
world,
On our thin layer of history,
However high up on tiptoes we can reach,
In family lore,
In a trophy case,
In the credits list,
In next century's textbooks.

Mostly,
It's the hunch we're not around long.
We just want someone to know we were here
And to like us back.

We've outgrown our nurseries,
And sought out new playgrounds,
Mountains and mansions,
Skyscrapers, stadiums,
Coffee shops, gymnasiums.

More of the world is ours to conquer.
More tools to carve our statement.
More crowds to compete.
More hurdles to our striving.

Chris Rice

It's not so easy anymore
To leave a noticeable mark.

I'll be truly fine
If it all turns out
That my best marks
Were made with crayons.

Chris Rice

Mercy and Judgement

In frequent moral debate
One name ever appears
As epitome and cliché
Of human evil.

Two questions I dare:
What hell would you devise for the Führer?
And most daring,
What heaven for him if mercy wins?

To declare his guilt is simple and right.
In this we judge fit
For guilt applies to all—
This thumps my chest—all includes me.

But what of my guilt to his?
Do I equally sin?
I do not find the scale.
Save that in a single way all sins are level—
They all defy equal Holiness.
Our self-compare, then,
Must only be to Him.
Not to the Führer,
Not to any other.

'I am not that bad'
Is to say
'God is not that holy.'
I am only true in saying,

Chris Rice

'I am not that good.'

I leave to Fairest Father our sentences.
And hope to God for all our sakes
That even a Hitler, if he should seek,
Would find mercy that overflows.
For if any man's sin could outweigh God's
mercy,
Who of us could trust in it?

My double ears receive their
Scolding contradictions.
In one, "How dare you overlook such evil!"
In the other, "How doubt you such mercy?"

My capacity fails me in all,
And bolts me toward my only hope,
To mercy that overflows!

I do not say he either sought or found it.
Only that I too need mercy to be so great a
flood!
And we who read
Have yet the time to seek it.
Lord, have mercy.

Chris Rice   115

We Rarely Die

We rarely die in meaningful ways,
With close-up camera shots,
Profound last words whispered,
While soft-lit misty beads trickle and glint
Across our cooling brows.
We mostly slip out
Unaware that it has happened.

Why do we first and always ask 'how did she
die?'
First, because we need to know
Which cruel enemy robbed us of her.
But we also ask because it is easier
answered—
She succumbed to such-and-such,
Like all of us have, or will.

Do not let the ways we die be our definitions!
Let us ask the better question,
'How did she live?'
And better yet,
(For you who yet read and breathe)
How are you living?

Let it be said of you, my dear reader,
When you are circled,
'Ah, this one died from living!'
We rarely live in meaningful ways.

Chris Rice

Upon Reading Wordsworth's Ode

The poet sounds sweet times, before our draft
Of Lethe's drops dissolved to drowsy dream
Bright glories 'ere our kinder earthly days.
Soft echoes lingered while our toddling self

Learned gradual of its fixed staticity,
Soon faded into boyish glint, then gone.
He so laments such unrecovered loss
And tries to trace in its fleet memory

Back-gazing reason now to conjure praise.
How true the poet wrings my longing forth!
And dredges up such melancholy ache!
Though gives it unremembered history's
name.

I'm humbled 'neath his masterful parle!
His splendid words and thoughts 'too deep for
tears.'
I feel them like, but frame them differently,
And if I may, I offer mirror's view:

The echo comes before the sound itself.
And not 'There was a time,' but There Will
Be.

Chris Rice   117

Every Bed

Every bed empties
Except our last.
Though it is mostly empty too!
Naked from these bed clothes
Our souls have flown
Finally and forever
Awake.

Chris Rice

Catharsis

I warn you, reader,
Do not read too much of this poet
Between his lines.

He's rehearsed at working words
In heftier ways than most.
He owns both intent and tools to move you.
He'll press your bruise to make it hurt.
He'll conjure sentiment from vacancies.

These tears you read in me are but your own.
They trail *your* cheeks, not mine.
These smiles my gentle lines flush to your
face
Are of *your* sweet memories!
It is my art and privilege
To aid them into view
By telling fibs
To lure you into truth.

That's not to say
I have no tear or memory of my own,
I do, but I don't tell them direct.
I tell them slant for Emily,
I heighten their pity and terror for Aristotle,
I contort my pose before I chisel it out for
Michelangelo!

Chris Rice   119

So I admit that I inflate, but to an artful end:
To tease up your past for its second work.
To agitate and stir.
To comfort or disturb.
To guide you by chain or twine or trick
To your catharsis.

So don't seek the poet in his lines
But yourselves.

He holds his poems out to you
Not as windows,
But mirrors.

Chris Rice

Waking

When I hear a man died in his sleep
I wonder a thing
Which no one alive
Can ever know—
What was it last he dreamed?

Then—
How long to realize he was no longer
dreaming?
What faces greeted him?
What silence there, or what music?
What utterance unplanned?
What unimagined sensations?
Did his eyes suddenly pop open
To a bright new room?
Or was it gradual
Like a child exchanging
With his grandpa
A penny for a dime
One at a time
Until they'd reached a million
And only then it dawned
With surprise
That his copper pile
Had changed to silver?

Chris Rice   121

Black Hole

Black hole,
Where darkness seems for now to win,
We wait you out.
You can't forever hold all that's sucked in
By your greedy gravity.
Your prisoned light will pack so tight
And in its time
Under its self-crushing weight
Gather strength and burst itself free
And shatter you to pieces
And shine back on you what you truly are.
Then we too will know.
Then we too are free.

Chris Rice

The Importance of Maps

Tell your story.
But don't leave out the map.
Draft it up at least in your mind
To keep your bearings
Or find a better way of telling.

Is there a stroll-along creek,
A mythic river?
Give her a name.
Perhaps you must cross, so how?
What compels your crossing?
Fear on this side, love on the other?
Is she icy-clear, ankle-deep?
Does she roil opaque and muddy like stew,
Deep and swift with upstream's history,
Or overstuffed with downstream's dread?
What villain lurks along her banks?
What lonely bower to find your peace?

Now what of this road?
Is it grass or gravel, paved or potholed?
Will you walk, limp, or ride on it?
Do other paths join or interrupt?
You need to know,
For your tale takes meaning with each
decision,
With every stranger who might be crossed
hereon.

Chris Rice

123

What about your borders?
Is your story wholly within maps' edges?
Or does a mystery loom unmapped beyond
To haunt and cloud your choices?

Is your map self-conscious
Of that gaping blank space
Perhaps dead center
Where none has ventured?
I dare you wander into its void.
Brave whatever is there.
Fill the gap.
Finish the map.
Color in the white emptiness
With local legend, monster or magic.

Is your map fresh, bright, colorful?
Or torn and drab, age-dingy,
On crumbly, dusty, musty parchment?
Or, better, was it inked by your hero
In his very own blood
On the uprolled skin of a wild she-boar
He trapped and gutted to survive the winter?
Yes, get that specific.

Lastly, is there a treasure
Marked there for the finding?
What cliff guards it?
What moat or cave?
Who deserves its riches?
Who does not?

Chris Rice

All I know is this—
If there is no map,
There is no treasure in your story.

Every story happens somewhere.
Don't forget your map.

Cause

The embers are too quiet,
The water too still.
I want, no,
Need
To move things.
To poke a stick in the coals,
To plop a stone in the lake.
To set a spark, a ripple.
To compel a crackle, a splash.
To know I made something, anything,
Happen.

Chris Rice

First Stone

He knelt to scratch unspoken words
In crusty dirt.

He coaxed my eyes away from her
And to myself.

I dropped my stone and backed away
And wandered home.

Chris Rice

The Innocence of Innocence

Innocence knows not itself
Until that day it dies,
Then rouses self-aware,
Only too late, and gone like a dream.

Echo fades where music played,
Like phantom swapped for real,
What is for what used to be,
Then doubts it ever was.

We had it only when we knew not,
Now long for what can never be again.
Had we only known, we sigh.
Had we only known.

Chris Rice

Flaunt

There is a Grace that pulses wild in universes'
veins.
There is a Strength that flicks aside ten
thousand hurricanes.
There is a Glory, double floods and drowns
all ocean shores.
And Love! Ah! Dante's 'love that moves the
sun and other stars!'

There is a Beauty better hid—undraped
would terrorize.
(In part, it's Kindness sets the angels distant
from our eyes.)
There's Mercy which annihilates! And Light
all blackness crushes!
And there is Life so unrestrained its blood
forever gushes!

So I believe, so kneel and flaunt my fragile
incompleteness
And gulp these bits of air to sing and celebrate
in weakness.

Chris Rice   129

Sunlight

"Let there be light!" he said.
How soon we shut it out
With clunky stones and musty roofs
To block his generous sky.
Our steeples point to it, though sadly out of
view
While we huddle beneath them,
Under false lights, with dimmers down,
Preaching 'Imposing darkness sets the better
mood to contemplate.'

What? Mood?
Thank God our children haven't lived enough
For us to teach out their inner lights!
They play and pray in simultaneity.
They belch and giggle on stiff pews
While mothers shush and pinch
And fathers glare at such irreverence.

What? Irreverence?
I dare say God smiles with the children
And winks at them,
Strokes their cheeks,
Strums their hair!
Then snorts and thumps the backs of grouchy
old heads
To say "Lighten up!
Throw your doors and windows open to the
sky.

Chris Rice

Your steeples are fine,
But come out from under them.
See and hear my happy birds sing,
Dazzled by my sparkling sun!"

The Universe Is Bent

The universe is bent
On killing us.
Trees are things
Just waiting to fall on people.
Unseen germs
Crawl every surface,
Swarm the vapor of every warm breath,
Pry their way into our blood
And rob life.
Sharks lurk,
Storms rip,
Terra quakes,
Monster waves smash and drown,
And (oh no!)
Asteroids the size of castles
Scream through silent space
In our direction
With dead aim.

Then why does every crack sprout something
green?
Why does every drop of every river teem?
Why, then, does one oceaned globe
Spin life-filled on its subtle tilt in hostile space
Which either burns or freezes everything else?

Because there is Grace after all!
The bent of the cosmos
Is not to snuff us out,

Chris Rice

But to frame us
Like a masterpiece.
To show that we,
Against all odds,
Matter.

Bucket List

One rattles on wobbly wheels
Shoved around with a mop
Sloshing gray pungent water
Smearing ammonia footprints
And curvy wide sideways brushstrokes
On a floor no cleaner than before.

One waits gaping beneath an udder
And sings its metal cadence
With each squeeze of the farmer's hand
Until it fills and foams into
A new and sweeter song.

One is knotted to the crank
And lowered to that place
Where sun has never played
Then draws back up with splashes
Of crystal liquid life
For the village to survive another day.

One is plastic neon
With a spade to match
For the floppy-hat toddler
To load with sand
Turn upside-down
And pretend castles happen easily.

Chris Rice

Spring

She peeks and hides
She peeks and hides
She can't decide
She can't decide
But tempts the crocus into bloom
Like maidens blush—
Not quite enough
But just enough
To make young lovers swoon.
The sunlight swims
A rolling patch of warm,
The air moves slight,
The cloud runs double fast
To pass its tiny chills across our limbs.
The city spills itself out onto porches
Bright sidewalks host their happy-calm
parades
Of strollers, runners,
Friends and lovers
Rediscovered.
See, chatty girls who walk in pairs
And flip their hair
For boys who strain their necks to stare.
Their glances collide,
Push upward smiles to brinks of lips,
Like the almost-blooms beneath their boots.
How soon the fields will rumble, bumble—
Bees and buds,
All bees and buds

Chris Rice

With tiny hints of green,
The slightest hints of green.
Ah, the world is lovesick again!

Chris Rice

When I Survey

When I survey
It's not the wood
Where I linger,
But on his toes.

Some thirty years before
Toes wiggled warm in a splashy womb,
And eager pressed against her skin
From inside.

Soon splashed atop the chilly waves
Of stormy Galilee,
Then squished in gooey Jordan's mud
While purest dove descended.

Toes, to keep his balance,
Gripped the splintered hulls of boats
And taught fishermen to cast their nets
In new directions!

Toes, reached for by crawling babes,
And he said, "Let them come,
For this is what the kingdom's like!"

Toes, tickled dry by a harlot's hair
Whose tears and perfume poured
While onlookers grumbled aloud
For she had sinned extravagantly
But found tonight where grace abounds!

Chris Rice   137

And just last night
These toes spread tight
Against an upper floor
Where he knelt and patted dry
The fresh rinsed toes of others—
Even one who would deny,
And one who would betray!

These toenails
Scraped and clawed in agony
Against the dirt beneath the olive trees
And begged a cup to pass.

And now
On a hill known for its skulls
Toes, pinned against a wooden beam
By spike? By sin?
No, by love.

When I survey
It's not the wood I count,
But toes!
Now stained of earth he made
And dripping red of deity.

Chris Rice

INDEX OF TITLES AND FIRST LINES:
(*Titles appear in italics.*)

A Lost Art 56
A word spoken 87
Adorned 97
Ah, first creature, first gift, 36
Ah, silly children! 69
An empty boat 44
Are the world's best minds in our past? 70
Birthday 104
Black Hole 122
Black hole,/Where darkness seems for now to win, 122
Borrowed 94
Bread Wine and Water 7
Bucket List 134
Catharsis 119
Cause 126
Clues 72
Create, create, create! 3
Crib 10
Crowded starlings pick clean the yard. 90
Curtains 20
Dead Poets 13
December 12 62
Do Not Write Me Larger Than I Am 63
Do not write me larger than I am. 63
Doubter's Prayer 101
Drawn to the shore again and shoeless, 82
Dying Alone 92
Edges 66
Even as a youngster I wondered— 103
Even as I toddled half a century past, 16
Even our windows to the soul 20
Every Bed 118
Every bed empties 118

Exhausted Poet 35
Fame Is An Africanized Bee 31
First Flake 6
First Memory 55
First Stone 127
Flaunt 129
Float into my field first flake of the year. 6
Fresh from the brothel 43
Grace 69
Grass points poke and tickle 10
For God's sake, don't drown in it! 54
Hangover 33
He asked the earless air 92
He knelt to scratch unspoken words 127
Her hair not silver but fool's gold 48
Her shoulder twitches loose the damned fly 29
Hindsight 103
Hoarder 95
How cliché. 13
I Aimed An Arrow Inward 5
I aimed an arrow inward 5
I can barely crawl 95
I cannot decide which is more impossible, 88
I disobeyed my father's frequent warnings, 106
I found my life on the edge of seasons 66
I saw you stand and pointing down, 97
I stopped and overheard the river talk 76
I warn you, reader, 119
I Was Just Thinking 96
I was just thinking 96
I Was Larger When a Child 45
I was larger when a child 45
I Wear My Favorites Out 16
I will build my cabin on a river 1
I wish he had said it— 7
I woke before them all. 33
If I were blind I still would know the sun, 15

If time could lapse before my eyes 65
Impossibility Theory 88
In a broth of brainish chemistry 111
In frequent moral debate 114
In that sleep before birth 27
Innocence knows not itself 128
It started in kindergarten 21
Just Kids 112
Kindergarten 21
Language is a lovely mystery! 81
Let there be light!" he said. 130
Lies 32
Life Science 27
Like an exasperated child 78
Like being stabbed without a dagger 61
Live To Be A Thousand 18
Love taunts death, 4
Low light hums dim 55
Mercy And Judgement 114
My age recounts his early days 26
My Devils Sing 91
My devils sing it thus: 91
My infant self did not choose immaturity, 18
My palm pressed hard against the rock 51
Neigh 29
No More 43
Nostalgia 26
Oak In October 99
Oh, my dear Emily, 31
On my chilly Thursday ramble, 99
On Time 36
One rattles on wobbly wheels 134
One-Piece Puzzles 44
Optimist 73
Our Best Minds 70
Over and over/Tell your kid he is a failure 108
Painter's Tantrum 78

Perfection 47
Pillow Math 75
Please, don't read me out loud. 38
Psalm Eighty-Eight-and-a-Half 61
Quite unaware those ancestors beneath 94
Rain 23
Rich Old Lady 48
River Of Time 1
River Talk 76
Rude morning dawns—I lie here half-awake 75
Same two hands 32
She peeks and hides 135
Should that rainbow crack, 73
Shy Poem 38
Sky, The Word 58
Sky, the word, is too, too small. 58
Slow Explosion 65
So blessed today my grateful knee to bend. 104
Soul 111
Spring 135
Squirrel Chase 4
Stages 11
Starlings 90
Sunlight 130
Tell your story. 123
Tend 8
The air is gray, but not entirely. 23
The embers are too quiet, 126
The Feel of Words 109
The Importance of Maps 123
The Innocence of Innocence 128
The jet's quiet, steady growl 28
The Language of Crows 40
The News 108
The Poet Interrupts 85
The poet interrupts my Now 85
The poet sounds sweet times, before our draft 117

The Universe Is Bent 132
The universe is bent/On killing us. 132
Then Sings My Soul 51
There is a Grace that pulses wild in universes' veins. 129
This morning I understood 40
Those crayon marks 112
Thoughts are swiftest. 35
To Sun Moon And Men 106
Too Much I Love 110
Too much I love this world you made! 110
Undertones 28
Unexplainable 81
Upon Reading Wordsworth's Ode 117
Waking 121
Warm 15
Waves 82
We always know where Pop is. 56
We Rarely Die 116
We rarely die in meaningful ways. 116
We think of times outside our own. 72
We wake up center stage, 11
What to Do with Guilt 54
When I hear a man died in his sleep 121
When I Survey 137
When I survey/It's not the wood 137
When we impose across our cityscapes 47
Who Has Summered At The Beach 24
Who has summered at the beach 24
Widen 3
Words 87
Words are like wappled voistures. 109
Wrap tight your sweater, closer still, 62
You Cannot Prove 79
You cannot prove 79
You knew we'd come to this! 101
Your soul is a small patch of Eden, 8

About the Author

Chris Rice grew up in the Maryland suburbs of Washington, D.C., the son of bookstore owners. After university-hopping for his B.A. degree in Psychology and Communication, he relocated to Nashville, TN in 1985 to pursue a songwriting career, which led him to record six studio albums and five specialty albums to date. He has since toured in all 48 contiguous states, and enjoyed more than a dozen Top Ten radio hits in the U.S. and abroad. He continues songwriting and other writing forms, and recently added painting to his artistic endeavors, having already sold over 150 original paintings in art shows and online. His residence and painting studio boast their proximity to some of the finest coffee shops and burger joints in Tennessee. When not writing or painting, Chris can be found rock climbing on hundred-foot cliffs around the Southeast.

Made in the USA
Charleston, SC
06 March 2016